Rediscovering Your Roots:

An Informational Guide to Finding Your Ancestors

This book is dedicated to all persons

desiring to rediscover their roots.

- Subrena C, Bowers

Table of Contents

Introduction: In Search of Us 1

Chapter One: Library of Congress 9

Chapter Two: Ancestry.com 21

Chapter Three: 23andMe 29

Chapter Four: African Ancestry 37

Chapter Five: NARA 57

Chapter Six: Oral Histories 77

Chapter Seven: Navigating Challenges 83

Chapter Eight: Guided by Ancestral Whispers 89

Chapter Nine: Collecting Artifacts 93

Chapter Ten: Sharing Your Story 97

Disclaimer Statement: Researcher's Responsibility and Risk Acknowledgment

The details in this document are here to teach and share knowledge only. We are not giving any advice. This means you shouldn't use this information instead of talking to experts like genealogists or other reliable sources. We tried our best to make sure the information in this document is correct and comes from trustworthy sources, but we can't be blamed for mistakes or for what happens when you use this information. You use this information at your own risk.

Rediscovering Your Roots: An Informational Guide to Finding Your Ancestors explains various tools that are made available to those seeking to reconnect to their ancestral roots. This book empowers you with the tools to delve deeper, reach further, and accomplish your research goals with purpose and clarity. Your passion for uncovering the past, coupled with the guidance within these pages, will undoubtedly illuminate the path to understanding your lineage.

Rediscovering Your Roots Collection

To enhance your exploration, consider embracing the complete trilogy: ***Rediscovering Your Roots: Step-by-Step Guide***, and ***Rediscovering Your Roots: Interviewer's Workbook*** work together to form an ensemble designed to maximize your journey of self-discovery.

To order the rest of the Rediscovering Your Roots collection, ***scan*** the Instagram QR code on the "Let's Get Social page which is directly after page 112.

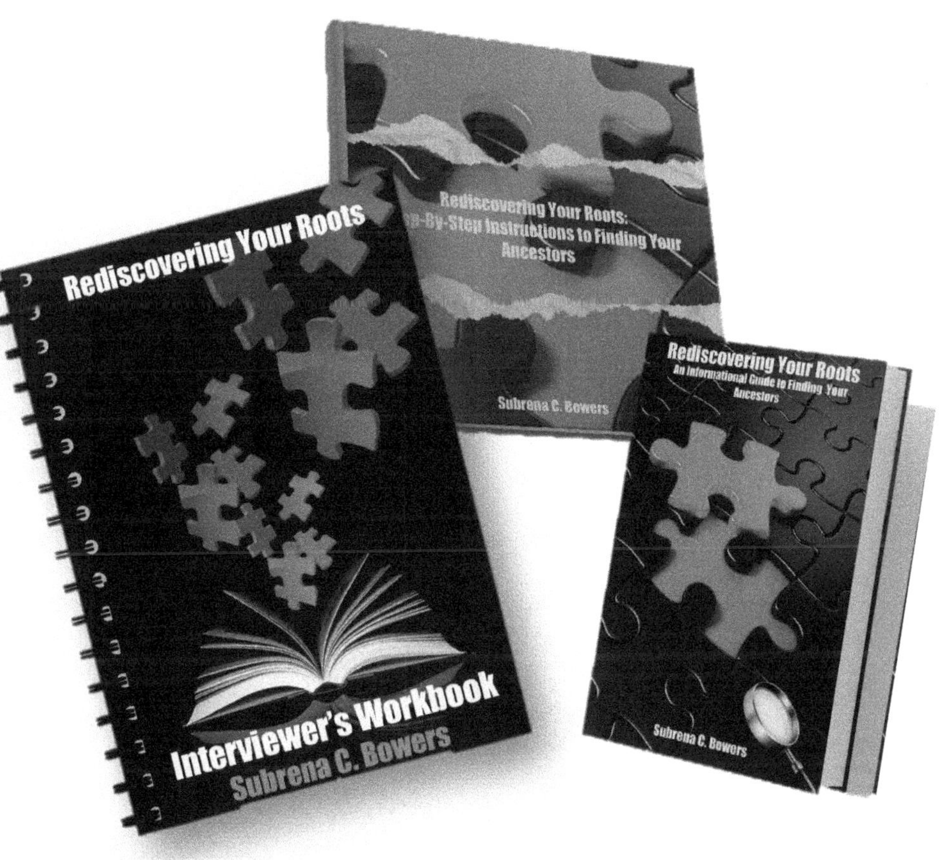

Introduction: In Search of Us

The Journey Begins

Preliminary Research Tips start on page 2 of the Rediscovering Your Roots Companion Guide.

Dear seeker of stories, you're not alone in your journey. While the pursuit of genealogy can become a passionate pursuit, remember that it's a testament to your love for your roots. Find that balance between the past and the present and let the stories you uncover enrich your life without overshadowing the vibrant stories still unfolding around you.

Welcome, family historians, to a journey that dances between the past and the present, where whispers of ancestors and echoes of history intertwine. As you dive into the realm of genealogy, know that you're not alone in this adventure. I'm here to share stories, insights, and a dash of magic to guide you through the captivating world of discovering your heritage.

Imagine sitting on your couch, eyes glued to the screen as celebrities on shows like "Finding Your Roots" and "Who Do You Think You Are?" trace their roots across time. Their journeys inspire you, reminding you that behind the veneer of the present lies a tapestry of stories waiting to be discovered. It's as if they're showing you that this treasure hunt is within your reach, too.

Just like you, I was captivated by those TV shows, witnessing celebrities reconnect with their family's past. Their emotional journeys resonated deeply, and I found myself yearning to embark on a similar quest. Could I, an ordinary person, trace my roots as they did? The answer was a resounding yes.

Before my genealogical adventure began, I could only trace my family tree back to my great grandmother. Like a puzzle missing pieces, my ancestry felt incomplete. But then I took that first step, and oh, what a journey it has been. With every record uncovered, every ancestor's name discovered, the tapestry of my Indigenous African heritage unfolded.

I'll let you in on a secret: I can now trace my family back to the late 1700s. Can you believe it? From humble beginnings, my ancestors' stories emerged like constellations in the night sky, painting a vivid picture of their lives and struggles. And you, dear reader, have the same potential to unravel the threads that tie you to your heritage.

So, fasten your seatbelt and get ready to traverse time. Let's explore the resources, the stories, and the magic that will lead you to your ancestors' doorsteps. With each step, you're not just unearthing the past; you're honoring your lineage, embracing your heritage, and becoming a storyteller for the generations to come. The journey is waiting – let's embark together!

My Story: My Genealogy Journey

In the heart of uncertainty, I embarked on a genealogy journey that promised to unveil the stories woven into the fabric of my family's past. It was a journey filled with anticipation, but also challenges I hadn't quite prepared for.

The Daunting Beginnings: Navigating the Unknown

As I took my first steps into the realm of genealogy, the path seemed shrouded in mystery. I knew my immediate family well, but the branches that extended beyond my own seemed like vast, uncharted territories. The task ahead felt daunting, the vastness of our family's history both thrilling and overwhelming.

Navigating Reluctance and Questions

I reached out to relatives outside of my immediate circle, hoping to piece together the puzzle of our shared heritage. Some seemed hesitant, questioning my motives, and wondering why I was so determined to delve into the past. I faced reluctant branches and skeptical faces, each with their reasons for their guardedness.

The Uncharted Waters of Family Dynamics

In my pursuit of roots, I encountered a spectrum of reactions. Some relatives were excited, some uninterested, while others regarded me with suspicion. Some held the position of family historians, safeguarding their own versions of history, and my inquisitiveness was met with unease. The notion of unveiling secrets and stories seemed to unearth dormant rivalries.

Challenges Faced and Lessons Learned

With unwavering patience and sensitivity, I embarked on a quest to mend bridges and build connections. I learned that family dynamics are as intricate as our genealogy itself, and my journey required not only researching documents but also delicately navigating relationships.

A Triumph of Dedication: The Fruit of Three Years

Three years of relentless research led me to a remarkable achievement – a three-volume compilation of my family's history. Filled to the brim with irrefutable facts, cherished personal stories, documents, and cherished photographs, these volumes painted a vivid portrait of our lineage through the tapestry of American history.

From History to Art: The Power of Storytelling

My passion transcended mere records. Inspired by the oldest documented Arkansas relatives, Cherry, and Wash Foote, I penned a nonfiction novel, *"The Cedar Chest."* This work breathed life into the stories of my ancestors, illuminating the lives they led and the trails they blazed.

From Page to Display: Leaving a Legacy

Through my perseverance, our family's history is slated to be a temporary exhibit in our state's premier African American cultural museum. The exhibit will showcase the narrative I have uncovered, inviting others to walk through our heritage and be inspired by our elders' lives.

WORDS OF WISDOM

The Allure of the Past: The Obsessive Trail of Genealogy

In the quest to trace the footsteps of our ancestors, the allure of the past can become a captivating obsession. The trail of genealogy winds through time, leading us to places unknown, stories untold, and connections we yearn to unveil. Yet, as the journey intensifies, the line between fascination and fixation can blur.

Hours transform into days, and days into weeks, as we pour over historical documents, sift through faded photographs, and scour archives in search of hidden tales. Every name, every date, every piece of evidence becomes a thread weaving a tapestry of history that feels like our own.

As our dedication deepens, family members may raise an eyebrow, wondering if we've delved too far into the past.

They might question why we've become consumed by names and dates, by stories that might seem long forgotten. They may see obsession where we see dedication. Don't be discouraged your persistence will pay off and they will thank you later.

It's important to acknowledge the fine line between passion and obsession. While delving into the annals of history can be fulfilling, there comes a point where it's wise to step back and reflect. Are we still connecting with the living, breathing individuals around us? Are we finding joy in the present as much as in the past?

Facing Discouragement: Staying True to the Journey

Despite the concerns of loved ones, don't let their skepticism discourage you. Remember that your dedication is an expression of love, curiosity, and a yearning to honor those who came before. Balance is key, but don't shy away from your pursuit of truth and connection.

In the end, the relentless search, the painstaking research, and the sleepless nights yield a reward that surpasses the challenges. You uncover stories that were waiting to be heard, legacies that were longing to be celebrated. Every effort transforms into a tribute to those who paved the way for your existence.

A Gentle Reminder: Cherishing the Present

As you traverse the path of genealogy, remember that the journey itself holds as much value as the destination. Embrace the connections you make with living relatives, and let your dedication serve as a bridge that unites the past and present.

Dear reader, let my journey serve as a testament to the power of unearthing the past and weaving it into the present. Challenges may arise, skepticism may loom, but every step is worth the knowledge gained. Through dedication and the art of storytelling, we can breathe life into our ancestors' whispers, leaving a legacy that resonates through generations.

Chapter One: Library of Congress

Unlocking History's Secrets

A list of needed tools to begin research starts on page 6 of Rediscovering Your Roots Companion Guide.

The Library of Congress, a treasure trove of knowledge and history, generously offers an array of free services that cater to the curious and the enthusiastic alike. From the comfort of your own home, you can access their vast digital collections, historical newspapers, and interactive exhibits without spending a dime.

The Library of Congress

Guess what? The Library of Congress (LOC) isn't just a place for dusty old books; it's a digital time machine! Their online treasure chest holds historical newspapers, photographs, and manuscripts that can teleport you to your ancestors' world. Let's decode handwritten letters, witness iconic moments through vintage photographs, and immerse ourselves in the past. Prepare to be awestruck by the tales you uncover and be patient with the process - after all, time travel can be a bit bumpy.

Library of Congress Website: Visit the official Library of Congress website to access their genealogy resources.

Website: www.loc.gov

Phone: 1-202-707-3399

Address: Library of Congress, 101 Independence Ave SE, Washington, DC 20540, USA

Costs: Access to the LOC digital documents, files and other <u>services are free.</u>

Imagine the LOC as a massive treasure chest filled with historical goodies. Each document is a glimpse into the lives of your ancestors.

Let's explore the types of documents you will find:

Newspapers: Your Personal Time Machine

Ever wished you could read a newspaper from a century ago? Well, guess what? You can! These newspapers are like time capsules, revealing what your great-great-grandparents read. Search for names, events, and places to get a feel for the times they lived in. You might even find a mention of your ancestors' birthdays or weddings – it's like eavesdropping on their conversations!

Pictures that Speak Volumes

Pictures are worth a thousand words, and these vintage photos are like portraits of your ancestors' lives. Look for images of the places they lived, the jobs they had, and the people they cherished. These photos are like pages from a family album you never knew you had.

The Story in Manuscripts

Imagine holding a letter written by your great-great-grandmother. Manuscripts are like whispers from the past, sharing their hopes, dreams, and challenges. These are like pages from a diary, giving you a front-row seat to their thoughts and emotions.

Legal Documents and Deeds

Census records, land deeds, and wills are like secret scrolls that tell tales of property, ownership, and family connections. It's like discovering hidden treasure maps that lead you to your ancestors' footsteps.

Military Records: Brave Ancestors

Military records are like badges of honor worn by your brave ancestors. Discover their service, battles fought, and even medals earned. These records remind you that your family has a legacy of courage.

Certificates and Records Galore

Marriage certificates, birth certificates, death certificates – oh my! These are like official certificates that mark the milestones of your ancestors' lives. Think of them as stamps in their personal history passports.

—◆—

For African American Readers

As a descendant of enslaved individuals, you're embarking on a quest to uncover the stories that time tried to erase. So, let's step into the past, armed with knowledge and determination!

Imagine the Library of Congress as a bridge to the past, a place where stories wait to be discovered. Once you're on their website, prepare to be amazed by the resources at your fingertips. For those tracing their roots as descendants of enslaved individuals, know that records prior to 1870 can be scarce. But fear not, for there are still tales waiting to be told.

In the pages of history, there exists a chapter marked by the silence of names, a chapter that tells the tale of formerly enslaved people who were not listed by name on slave schedules. This absence, a reflection of a painful past, echoes through time, reminding us of the countless individuals whose identities were relegated to the shadows.

As we journey back, we encounter the 19th-century U.S. Federal Census, a document that holds stories etched in numbers and categories. The slave schedules, born from a system that dehumanized, often left the names of those who endured unspeakable hardships unspoken. Instead, they were recorded as numbers, gender markers, ages, and a mere shadow of their essence.

In the face of this, the quest to uncover the identities of our ancestors takes on new depth. It becomes an endeavor fueled by empathy and a desire to give voice to those who were denied it. So, how do we bridge this gap? How do we reach across the chasm of history to connect with those who were denied their rightful place in records?

We embrace the clues hidden within those schedules, the markers that reveal the lives lived and the stories yearning to be known. Age and gender may hint at family structures. The locations of plantations or farms can unveil ties to known owners. In glimpses of ages and sex, we find the thread that links one individual to another, painting a portrait of kinship.

We turn to wills and probate records, seeking any reference to individuals who may have transitioned from enslavement to freedom. Newspapers from that era might yield valuable insights, shedding light on individuals' pursuits and accomplishments. In the absence of names, we craft a mosaic of existence, one fragment at a time.

This journey is not just an exploration of the past; it's a journey of connection, compassion, and reclamation. As we weave together the strands of information, we breathe life into the numbers, transforming them into the names that were once lost.

Let us tread softly as we honor those who walked a path marked by hardship and resilience. Let us remember that behind each entry on a schedule, there beats a heart, dreams, and a spirit yearning to be acknowledged. In our quest to unveil their stories, we offer a tribute to their enduring legacy, and we recognize that every effort to restore their names is a step toward healing a historical wound.

Embrace the Fragments

For many African Americans, tracing family history beyond 1870 can be like searching for fragments of a puzzle scattered by time. While records before this era are limited, each piece you uncover is a triumph. Imagine each document as a treasure chest that holds clues to your ancestors' lives. Every detail matters, whether it's a name, a location, or a seemingly insignificant date.

Building a Story with Census Records

Census records are like snapshots of history, freezing moments in time. For those tracing their roots, the 1870 census is like a milestone. It's the first one that lists formerly enslaved individuals by name. Imagine seeing your great-great-grandparents' names for the first time, like echoes from the past that resonate in your heart.

Land Deeds and Stories of Freedom

Land deeds are like footprints left behind by your ancestors. They show where they owned land and built lives after emancipation. Comb through these records and let them guide you to the places your family once called home. Their stories of freedom are etched in these pages, waiting for you to give them voice.

Birth, Marriage, and Death Records

Birth certificates, marriage licenses, and death records are like chapters in the book of your family's legacy. These documents might emerge as the pages of your ancestors' lives after their emancipation. Imagine discovering the marriage certificate of your great-great-grandparents, a testament to their love and determination.

While the collection is vast, here are some types of records and resources that you can find within the LOC:

African American Newspapers:

The Library of Congress holds a collection of African American newspapers, both historical and contemporary. These newspapers provide insights into the lives, experiences, and perspectives of African Americans throughout history.

Manuscripts and Archives:

Manuscript collections contain letters, diaries, memoirs, and personal documents that can offer firsthand accounts of African American experiences. Look for collections related to civil rights activists, writers, and other notable figures.

Photographs and Prints:

The Library of Congress has a vast collection of photographs and prints that document the history and culture of African Americans. These images provide visual records of individuals, events, and communities.

Oral Histories:

Oral history collections include recorded interviews and testimonies from African Americans who have shared their personal stories, memories, and experiences.

African American Sheet Music:

The Library's sheet music collection includes African American music compositions that reflect cultural and musical contributions.

Congressional Records and Documents:

Congressional records contain debates, speeches, and legislation related to African American history, civil rights, and social justice issues.

Printed Books and Reference Materials:

The Library of Congress houses a comprehensive collection of books, reference materials, and scholarly publications on African American history, culture, and genealogy.

Maps and Atlases:

Maps can provide insights into historical African American communities, migration patterns, and neighborhoods.

Online Digital Collections:

The Library of Congress offers online digital collections that include photographs, manuscripts, newspapers, and other resources related to African American history and genealogy.

Exhibitions and Events:

The Library often hosts exhibitions, lectures, and events that focus on African American history, literature, and culture.

Online Research Guides:

The Library of Congress provides research guides and resources specifically tailored to African American genealogy and history.

Keep in mind that the Library of Congress is continually expanding its collections and resources related to African American history. When researching, make sure to explore their catalog, online databases, and special collections to uncover valuable records that can enrich your understanding of African American heritage.

My Story: Unveiling Resilience

As a descendant of formerly enslaved people, my journey was a mix of excitement and heartache. The records prior to 1870 were like whispers, but they revealed glimpses of strength and resilience. Each name, each place, was like a connection to the past that I was determined to honor.

Imagine visiting a place your ancestors once called home. I visited my family's land, and as I stood there, I could almost hear their voices carried by the wind. The stories that emerge from these places are like tributes to the resilience of your ancestors. You're not just reading history; you're living it.

For many descendants of enslaved individuals, oral histories become lifelines to the past. Elders pass down stories that weren't written in official records. These tales are like hidden treasures waiting to be discovered. Listen closely as your grandparents share their memories; these moments are like threads that weave the tapestry of your history.

Your journey into the past is unique, and as a descendant of enslaved individuals, you're reclaiming the narratives that were obscured. Celebrate every discovery, no matter how small. Whether you find stories in documents, in land, or in whispers from the past, remember that you're weaving together a narrative of strength and resilience. Your ancestors' stories are waiting to be told, and you're the storyteller who will give them the voice they deserve.

Keep digging, keep connecting, and keep celebrating the rich tapestry of your African American heritage. Your journey has just begun, and every revelation is a step toward understanding yourself, your family, and the remarkable history you all share. Happy genealogy hunting!

Chapter Two: Ancestry.com

Unraveling the Digital Realm

Step-by-Step Instructions about using Ancestry.com starts on page 10 of Rediscovering Your Roots Companion Guide.

You're diving into the world of genealogy, and Ancestry.com is your trusty compass. Ready to uncover your family's secrets? Set up your account and start your journey today.

Ancestry.com

Ancestry.com is like a magical key that opens doors to your personal history. The documents you find – birth certificates, marriage records, and census data – are the puzzle pieces that complete the picture of your ancestry. These pieces connect you to a larger narrative, a narrative in which you play an integral role. Your roots run deep, and the knowledge of your heritage can empower you to embrace your identity with newfound pride.

Ancestry.com is a comprehensive genealogy platform that offers a wide range of resources for researching your family history.

Contact Information:

Website: www.ancestry.com

Phone Number: 1-800-ANCESTRY (1-800-262-3787)

For specific inquiries or assistance, it's advisable to explore their website's "Contact Us" or "Support" section to find additional contact options and resources.

Ancestry.com offers different membership plans with varying features and access levels. Please keep in mind that specific features, access to records, and membership benefits can vary based on the membership level you select. Pricing can change over time, and there might be promotions or discounts available, so it's recommended to visit their official website for the most up-to-date pricing information to find the plan that best suits your research needs and budget.

As a general guideline, <u>Ancestry.com membership plans might range from around \$19.99 to \$49.99 per month</u>, depending on the plan you choose. They might also offer annual subscriptions at a slightly discounted rate compared to the monthly plans.

Once you have picked your plan, it's time to start your research! With each click and search, you're not just delving into names and dates, but breathing life into your family's legacy. Every ancestor has a story, a life rich with experiences, dreams, and resilience. As you peel back the layers of time, you might uncover the tenacity of a great-great-grandparent who overcame challenges, the courage of a distant relative who ventured into the unknown, or the wisdom of those who held your family's values close to heart.

As you dive into the past, don't be surprised if you find pieces of yourself in the stories you uncover. Perhaps you'll discover shared interests, similar physical traits, or a common determination that's been passed down through generations. This realization can be an inspiring reminder that you are a continuation of a remarkable journey, a torchbearer of your family's history.

The road to your ancestors may have twists and turns, but each discovery is a step forward. The connections you make with your past can extend to your present, offering insight and guidance in navigating the complexities of life. Your ancestors' strength can be a wellspring of motivation, reminding you that resilience and determination are part of your genetic makeup.

So, fellow historian, let Ancestry.com be your vessel on this remarkable expedition. Embrace the thrill of discovery, the excitement of unearthing forgotten stories, and the pride of carrying your heritage forward. With each piece of the puzzle you find, you're not just piecing together the past – you're forging a deeper connection to yourself and those who came before you. Your journey awaits – happy uncovering!

To help you in your efforts, here's a list of things you can typically find on Ancestry.com:

Census Records: Federal and state census records that provide details about your ancestors' households, names, ages, relationships, occupations, and more.

Vital Records: Birth, marriage, and death records that offer essential information about your ancestors' life events.

Military Records: Military service records, draft registration cards, pension records, and more related to your ancestors' military involvement.

Immigration and Naturalization Records: Passenger lists, immigration records, and naturalization documents revealing details about your ancestors' journey to a new country.

Newspaper Archives: Historical newspaper articles that can provide insights into your ancestors' lives, events, and community involvement.

Cemetery and Burial Records: Information about burial locations, grave markers, and cemetery records.

Census Substitutes: Specialized records, such as city directories, voter lists, and tax records, can help fill in gaps between census years.

Family Trees and User-Submitted Content: User-generated family trees, photographs, stories, and documents shared by other Ancestry.com members.

School Records and Yearbooks: Educational records, yearbooks, and school-related documents that may provide information about your ancestors' academic experiences.

Land and Property Records: Deeds, land grants, and property-related documents that reveal your ancestors' land ownership and transactions.

Occupation and Employer Information: Records related to your ancestors' occupations, including employment records, trade directories, and professional associations.

Probate and Will Records: Documents related to wills, estate settlements, and probate proceedings that offer insights into your ancestors' final wishes.

Social Security and Voter Records: Social Security applications and voter registration records that provide additional information about your ancestors' lives.

Historical Maps and Gazetteers: Maps, atlases, and gazetteers that can help you visualize your ancestors' locations and understand the historical context.

Passport Applications and Travel Records: Passport applications, border crossings, and travel documents that shed light on your ancestors' journeys.

Occupational and Trade Directories: Directories that list your ancestors' professions, businesses, and roles in their communities.

DNA Matching and Ethnicity Estimates: DNA test results and matching with potential relatives based on shared DNA segments. Ethnic estimates offer insights into your ancestral origins.

With an AncestryDNA kit, you can discover more about your ethnic origins and **connect with relatives** who share parts of your DNA.

As you bring your journey with Ancestry.com services to a close, remember that you've embarked on a remarkable expedition into the tapestry of your past. With each click and discovery, you've bridged the gap between generations, unearthing the stories of those who came before you. The connections you've made, the roots you've uncovered, and the stories you've revealed have added new dimensions to your understanding of self and heritage.

As you move forward, carry the spirit of exploration and connection with you, knowing that your ancestors' stories are now interwoven with your own. Should you choose to continue your ancestral odyssey, consider exploring additional resources, engaging with community, and sharing your journey to inspire others.

The book of your ancestry is bound by the pages of history, and you hold the pen to continue writing the story.

Happy hunting, and may your legacy be as rich and vibrant as the history you've uncovered!

Chapter Three: 23andMe

It's In The Blood

23andMe processes are outlined beginning on page 16 of Rediscovering Your Roots Companion Guide.

Hey there, fellow historians of the unknown! Did you know that your DNA holds the key to connecting with relatives you might not even know exist? Brace yourselves, because we're diving into the fascinating world of finding unknown cousins using 23andMe — and trust us, it's a journey that might lead you to unexpected places and faces!

23andMe

Are you ready to embark on an exciting journey into your genetic heritage? Well, hold onto your DNA strands, because we're about to dive into the amazing world of 23andMe – a search engine that unveils the secrets of your genes and takes ancestry exploration to a whole new level!

Contact Information:

Website: www.23andme.com

Phone: 1-800-239-5230.

Customer Support: You can find customer support options on their website under the "Contact Us" or "Help Center".

Cost of 23andMe DNA Testing Kits:

The cost of 23andMe DNA testing kits can vary depending on the version of the kit you choose. They offer different packages that might include different features such as health reports and ancestry insights. As of my last update, the prices might range from around $99 to $199 for the basic kits. Please be aware that prices can change, and there might be discounts or promotions available, so I recommend checking their website for the most current pricing information.

What's the Buzz About 23andMe?

Did you know that your DNA can tell you stories about your ancestors – where they came from, what traits they passed down, and even potential health insights. That's exactly what 23andMe does! It's like a magical decoder ring for your genes, revealing tales that go back generations.

So, whether you're curious about your family's history, or you're simply intrigued by the secrets your genes hold, 23andMe is your ultimate guide to a journey of self-discovery.

Imagine if your genes could whisper stories about your family's past. Well, with 23andMe, they can! You might uncover relatives who share your DNA but have been lost in the folds of time. These cousins could be from different racial backgrounds, making your family tree more colorful than ever.

When you connect with unknown cousins through 23andMe, you might find that they come from different racial groups than you. This is like living proof that we're all part of one big human family, connected by our shared history.

Where in the World Are They?

Ready for the thrilling part? Not only can you find unknown cousins, but you can also see where they live! 23andMe offers a feature that shows you the locations where your DNA relatives call home. It's like getting a virtual passport to different corners of the world, all through the power of your genes.

A Sensitive Approach to Diversity

When you embark on this journey, it's important to approach it with an open heart and a sensitivity to different races and cultures. Embrace the beauty of diversity as you connect with cousins who might look different from you but share a common genetic thread.

How It Works

Getting started is as easy as 1-2-3. Just provide a small saliva sample, send it to 23andMe, and wait for the magic to unfold. Within weeks, you could be discovering cousins you never knew existed, from all walks of life. It's like uncovering hidden treasures in your family history!

MY STORY

A Heartwarming Tale: Finding Family with 23andMe

Once upon a time, in the land of genealogy, two cousins embarked on a journey of discovery that would forever change their lives. These cousins had always carried a hint of uncertainty about their family roots, questioning the paths that led to them. Little did they know that a simple DNA test on 23andMe would bring them the validation and connection they had been seeking.

Meet Terri and Elle: Longing for Answers

Terri and Elle had both grown up with lingering questions about their family lineage. They wondered about their heritage, their ancestors' stories, and the missing puzzle pieces that left gaps in their narratives. The genealogy bug had bitten them hard, and they yearned for a sense of belonging, a place where their family puzzle could finally come together.

A Glint of Hope on 23andMe

One day, Terri and Elle decided to take a leap of faith and send their DNA samples to 23andMe. Little did they know that this tiny action would lead to a heartwarming revelation. As they navigated through the results, something magical happened – they saw my profile, confirming that they were indeed connected to the family they suspected!

Tears of Joy and a Sense of Home

Upon discovering and validating their connection, Terri and Elle were overcome with emotions. They reached out to me. We exchanged messages, shared stories, pictures, and our shared excitement. As we spoke on the phone, our voices were laced with emotion and relief. Finally, the questions that had haunted them for years were answered. They weren't alone; they had a cousin who understood their journey, their longing, and their dreams.

A Feeling of Belonging

For Terri and Elle, the experience was more than just a DNA match. It was a sense of coming home, of finding a missing piece of themselves. We had a shared history, a shared family tree, and a shared sense of belonging. No longer were they adrift in the sea of uncertainty – they were anchored by the bond of blood and the power of our shared genetic heritage.

A Journey of Heartfelt Connection

Terri and Elle's story reminds us that family connections go beyond just names and dates. They hold the power to heal, to validate, and to create a sense of belonging that resonates deep within our hearts. Through the digital magic of 23andMe, we found one another, and they found a sense of completeness that had eluded them for so long.

In a world where we're all connected by threads of shared DNA, Terri and Elle's journey is a beautiful reminder that our roots run deep, and the bonds of family are a treasure that can never be underestimated.

As you stand at the intersection of your past and present, armed with the knowledge from 23andMe, remember that this journey is just the beginning. You've unlocked the door to a world of connections, understanding, and self-discovery.

The threads of your ethnicity weave into a diverse and vibrant tapestry, connecting you to cultures and stories that stretch across time. And those modern-day relatives? They're not just names on a screen; they're potential bonds waiting to be nurtured. Embrace this new chapter with open arms, for you now hold the power to build bridges that span generations.

As you move forward, let the richness of your heritage and the promise of these newfound relationships guide you. The story of you is still unfolding, and the pages are yours to write.

Embrace your roots, connect with your relatives, and let this newfound knowledge propel you toward a future illuminated by the light of your past!

Chapter Four: African Ancestry

---◆---

The Motherland

Instructions on how to access and utilize African Ancestry's services starts on page 20 of Rediscovering Your Roots Companion Guide.

Dear reader, isn't it amazing to uncover the threads that connect us to our roots? So, turn the page to dive even deeper into the enchanting world of our traditions, where every detail tells a story, and every ritual binds us to our heritage!

African Ancestry

African Ancestry Test Kits are designed to trace the ancestry of single lineages of the family tree. Trace your maternal line with the MatriClan Test. Trace your paternal line with the PatriClan Test. African Ancestry will identify the specific African country of origin and tribe that you share ancestry with during the past 500 - 2,000 years... if the result is African. **Note**: They have an assurance statement which states: *"We destroy your DNA - we do not sell or share it."*

Contact Information:

Website: www.africanancestry.com

Customer Support: support@africanancestry.com

Phone: 1 (202) 723-0900

Mailing Address:

5614 Connecticut Avenue NW, #297

Washington, DC 20015

Cost: <u>The cost for the MatriClan and PatriClan DNA kits cost $299.00.</u> However, please note that prices might have changed since this book was written. For up-to-date pricing information, I recommend visiting the official African Ancestry website or contacting their customer support.

What sets African Ancestry apart is its laser-focused dedication to connecting you with your African roots. While other DNA testing services provide broader ethnic percentages, African Ancestry goes deep, comparing your DNA to over 400 African ethnic groups. It's like a cultural GPS that guides you straight to your ancestral homeland.

Imagine standing on the threshold of history, gazing back through time to uncover the origins of your family's journey. African Ancestry.com offers you the chance to bridge the gap between your present and the distant past, connecting you with the cultures and traditions that are an integral part of who you are. This journey is more than a collection of facts; it's a soul-stirring experience that can ignite a profound sense of belonging.

Delve into the richness of your African ancestry as you trace your lineage to specific ethnic groups and regions. The insights gained from African Ancestry.com's database are more than mere data – they are windows into the diverse tapestry of African history. Reclaim the stories that have been whispered through the generations and celebrate the unity of your heritage.

Empower Yourself and Future Generations:

By embracing the knowledge of your African roots, you're not only honoring your ancestors' legacies but also empowering yourself and future generations. The strength and resilience that flow through your veins are the same qualities that have withstood the test of time. As you learn more about your origins, you can become a beacon of inspiration for your loved ones, fostering a connection that transcends time and distance.

Imagine tracing your heritage back to the very lands your ancestors called home. Now, imagine going back to Africa.

Touring African Countries

African Ancestry Tours offer an unforgettable experience that bridges the gap between past and present. As you step onto the African soil, you'll be enveloped in the rich tapestry of culture, history, and connection.

Your journey begins with the unveiling of your ancestral tribe through DNA testing. Armed with this newfound knowledge, you'll set foot in the vibrant landscapes of various African countries, where your heritage comes to life. From the rhythmic beats of local music to the flavors of traditional cuisine, every moment immerses you in the essence of your roots.

As you connect with distant cousins, share stories, and embrace the warmth of shared experiences, you'll realize that this journey is not just about the destination – it's about self-discovery and belonging. You'll return home with a heart full of memories, a mind enlightened by history, and a soul forever tied to the land that gave rise to your lineage.

African Ancestry Tours isn't just a trip; it's a transformational odyssey that allows you to honor your heritage, build connections, and weave your own story into the fabric of time. Go visit your ancestors' lands and let the spirit of Africa guide you on the voyage of a lifetime.

Unlock the door to your African heritage and let African Ancestry.com guide you toward a path of enlightenment, connection, and belonging. Your history is waiting to be rediscovered – take the first step today!

African American Traditions Tied to Africa

As we continue our journey, let's travel back in time to a chapter filled with stories of strength and resilience. The

diaspora, <u>a word that means the scattering of people across different lands</u>, brought African Americans far from their homeland, Africa. This journey, though painful, led to the creation of new stories, rich cultures, and beautiful traditions. Let's explore some of those contemporary traditions and look at its African roots.

Tattoos are Stories Etched in Skin

Imagine a world where skin becomes a canvas, where every tattoo tells a tale. African tribes like the Nuba and Maasai used tattoos to speak their stories. Stories were etched in skin, where memories, courage, and identity came to life. Tattooing is an ancient art practiced by African tribes like the Nuba and Maasai. These intricate designs were not just decorations; they held deep meaning. From marking life's milestones, marked moments of bravery, or etchings that celebrated achievements, tattoos are a living history etched onto skin.

Bald Heads: Artistry with a Message

Just like tattoos, the bald head has its own tale. In West Africa, the shaved head was often a sign of nobility and wisdom, and in some tribes, it marked a rite of passage into adulthood.

The Nuba people of Sudan are known for the practice of putting tattoos on their bald heads. Their tradition of adorning their bald heads with intricate tattoos is a unique cultural practice that holds deep significance within their community. These tattoos often carry symbolic meanings related to identity, status, and cultural heritage among the Nuba people.

Hairstyles that Tell Stories: Bantu Knots, and Braids

Imagine hairstyles that are more than just looks – they are stories whispered through time. Bantu knots, those cute and coiled knots, have their origins in the Bantu tribes of Central and Southern Africa. They celebrate the beauty of African hair while connecting us to our roots. Braids, those intricate patterns woven into hair, were a way for African tribes like the Fulani and Yoruba to tell stories of their identity and heritage.

Feasts of Culture: Food that Nourishes the Soul

The delicious flavors of African American cuisine are a fusion of memories from Africa. Dishes like gumbo, jambalaya, and collard greens are inspired by the food of West African tribes like the Wolof and Igbo. These flavors speak of resilience and creativity, making every bite a taste of the journey our ancestors took across the sea.

Dance and Music: The Rhythms of Ancestry

In the beat of a drum, the sway of a hip, we find the rhythm of our roots. The vibrant dance moves and infectious rhythms of African American dance and music hark back to dances like the Adowa of the Akan people and the Djembe drumming of West Africa.

Jewelry: Beyond Ornamentation to Culture

Jewelry is more than just decoration; it's a language of culture and identity. Among certain African cultures, nose rings held great significance. Tribes like the Berber and Beja saw them as expressions of beauty and a connection to heritage. These adornments spoke loudly about the wearer's history, bridging the gap between the past and the present.

Necklaces, bracelets, and other jewelry often featured materials from nature, tying wearers to the earth's beauty and their roots.

Rituals of Unity: Connecting Traditions

Step into a world of unity, where rituals bind hearts together. Just as African tribes performed rituals to honor life's moments, Black fraternities and sororities have their own unique traditions.

Imagine stepping into a circle of unity, surrounded by those who share your journey. Just as African tribes performed rituals to mark important moments, Black fraternities and sororities have their own special traditions. These mesmerizing rituals, like stepping, call and response, and secret handshakes, echo the practices of African tribes. They build bonds of brotherhood and sisterhood, preserving history while creating a bright future.

Certain rituals and traditions within Black fraternities and sororities in the United States are inspired by or tied to specific African cultures and tribes. While it's important to note that the details of these connections can vary and might not be universally agreed upon, here are a few examples:

1. Alpha Phi Alpha Fraternity, Inc.:

This fraternity, the first established for African Americans, is often associated with rituals inspired by ancient Egyptian culture. The use of symbols like the Great Sphinx of Giza and the pyramids, as well as references to African history and culture, are prevalent in their rituals.

2. Kappa Alpha Psi Fraternity, Inc.:

Kappa Alpha Psi draws inspiration from the culture and traditions of the Ashanti people of West Africa. The fraternity's founders incorporated aspects of Ashanti culture, such as the "fez" hats worn in homage to the Ashanti king's crown.

3. Omega Psi Phi Fraternity, Inc.:

Omega Psi Phi, known for its distinctive "ques" call and stylized branding, has drawn inspiration from various African cultures. While not directly tied to a specific tribe, their rituals and practices often reflect a celebration of African heritage.

4. Delta Sigma Theta Sorority, Inc.:

Delta Sigma Theta, one of the prominent Black sororities, has rituals inspired by African and Egyptian cultures. Their "Eleusinian Mysteries" initiation ritual incorporates symbols such as the pyramids and the sphinx, along with references to ancient African heritage.

5. Zeta Phi Beta Sorority, Inc.:

Zeta Phi Beta, another significant sorority, draws inspiration from the African heritage as well. While not tied to a specific tribe, their rituals and practices reflect a commitment to celebrating and preserving African American culture.

It's important to approach these connections with cultural sensitivity and understanding. While there may be influences from African tribes in these fraternity and sorority rituals, they have evolved over time within the context of African American culture and history. These connections often serve to honor and pay homage to African heritage while fostering unity, education, and empowerment within their respective organizations.

MY INSPIRATIONAL STORY

Amidst the stories of loss, there is a ray of hope that shines brighter than ever. African Ancestry, a company full of love and determination, is on a mission to help African Americans reconnect with their ancestral roots. Through the magic of DNA, they trace our lineage back to specific African tribes, reigniting the flame of connection that was almost lost.

Note: My African Ancestry testing results discovered I came from the Tikar people who are living in modern day Cameroon. I was elated when I received my certificate acknowledging my African ethnicity. Filled with excitement, I began researching facts about the Tikar culture and its influences on modern day African Americans.

The Tikar culture's echoes have resonated beyond Cameroon's borders, reaching the African diaspora. African Americans, in particular, have inherited elements of Tikar customs and practices. The art of storytelling, communal spirit, and a reverence for ancestral heritage are threads connecting the Tikar to their distant kin across the Atlantic.

As you uncover the secrets of your heritage and pinpoint the African tribe to which you belong through the magic of DNA kits, a whole new world of discovery awaits you. Imagine the thrill of standing on African soil, connecting with the land that once echoed with the footsteps of your ancestors. Your journey doesn't end with data and percentages; it begins with a renewed sense of identity, an unbreakable bond with a tribe that carries your legacy.

As a descendant of a formerly enslaved ancestor there are additional resources that you can access to help you rediscover ancestors. Let's explore the LOC for those that were once enslaved. The best place would be to look at the Freedmen's Bureau records.

Freedmen's Bureau & African American Records

The Freedmen's Bureau holds immense historical significance as a pivotal institution that played a crucial role in the aftermath of the American Civil War. Officially known as the Bureau of Refugees, Freedmen, and Abandoned Lands, it was established by Congress in 1865 to aid the millions of newly emancipated African American slaves and poor whites in the South during the Reconstruction era. The Bureau's impact extended far beyond its immediate operations, leaving a lasting legacy that continues to resonate in American history.

Here are some key details you might uncover using Freedmen's Bureau documents:

Names and Family Relationships:

Labor contracts and marriage records from the Freedmen's Bureau can provide names, ages, and relationships of individuals within your family. This can help you trace family connections and create a more accurate family tree.

Employment and Labor Agreements:

Labor contracts between formerly enslaved individuals and former enslavers can reveal details about your ancestors' work arrangements, wages, and the terms under which they were employed.

Education and School Records:

The Freedmen's Bureau established schools, and records from these institutions might include the names and ages of children attending, giving you insights into the education of your ancestors.

Land and Property Ownership:

The Bureau distributed land to freedpeople. Records related to land transactions can indicate whether your ancestors owned land, providing a link to their economic status and possible locations.

Medical and Healthcare Records:

Documents related to medical care might reveal health conditions, treatments, and medical services provided to your ancestors.

Marriage and Family Records:

Marriage records maintained by the Freedmen's Bureau can help you uncover information about your ancestors' marital status, spouse's name, and marriage date.

Letters and Correspondence:

Personal letters and correspondence with the Freedmen's Bureau might reveal personal stories, challenges, and requests for assistance made by your ancestors.

Requests for Aid and Assistance:

Requests for clothing, food, and other forms of aid can provide insights into the daily struggles and challenges your ancestors faced during the transition from slavery to freedom.

Testimonies and Personal Narratives:

Some individuals shared their personal narratives with the Freedmen's Bureau, offering firsthand accounts of their experiences during slavery, emancipation, and Reconstruction.

Community and Social Life:

Records related to church activities, social gatherings, and community events can shed light on the social life and interactions of your ancestors.

Location and Movement:

Documentation of where your ancestors lived, their movements, and any relocations can help you trace their journey and establish connections to specific areas.

Legal and Property Disputes:

Legal documents can include information about disputes over property rights, inheritance, and other legal matters that affected your ancestors.

Remember that the availability of specific records varies, and not all records might be fully intact. It's important to conduct thorough research and consult historical archives, genealogical websites, and repositories that house Freedmen's Bureau records to access these valuable documents and uncover the stories of your ancestors.

Through its records and correspondence, the Freedmen's Bureau left behind a rich archive that serves as a critical resource for researchers, historians, and genealogists seeking to understand the experiences of formerly enslaved individuals during Reconstruction.

While the Freedmen's Bureau faced challenges, including funding shortages and opposition from white supremacist groups, its efforts laid the groundwork for progress in civil rights and racial equality. It paved the way for subsequent generations to continue fighting for equal rights and social justice.

In essence, the Freedmen's Bureau represents an early attempt by the federal government to address the immense challenges faced by newly freed African Americans and to begin the process of racial equality and integration. Its impact can be seen in the educational, economic, and social advancements made by African Americans in the years that followed, and it remains an essential part of American history and the ongoing struggle for civil rights.

National Archives and Records Administration (NARA):

The National Archives holds a significant collection of Freedmen's Bureau records. You can visit the National Archives in person or access their online resources to search for specific records and documents.

FamilySearch:

FamilySearch, a genealogy website operated by The Church of Jesus Christ of Latter-day Saints, offers a substantial collection of Freedmen's Bureau records that are available for free. You can search and browse records online.

Contact Information:
Website: www.familysearch.org

Ancestry.com:

Ancestry.com has digitized and indexed a variety of Freedmen's Bureau records, making them easily searchable online. Access to these records requires a subscription.

Fold3:

Fold3, a website specializing in military records, also hosts a collection of Freedmen's Bureau records related to military affairs and claims. Some records are available for free, while others require a subscription.

Local and State Archives:

Many state and local archives have preserved copies of Freedmen's Bureau records that pertain to specific regions. These archives can provide valuable insights into the local context of your ancestors' lives.

Library of Congress:

The Library of Congress has a collection of Freedmen's Bureau records, including letters, reports, and other documents. Some of these materials are available online through their digital collections.

African American Genealogy Societies:

African American genealogy societies and historical organizations may have compiled resources and guides for accessing Freedmen's Bureau records specific to your region.

Local Libraries and Historical Societies:

Local libraries and historical societies in areas with significant African American communities may have access to Freedmen's Bureau records and other related materials.

Online Archives and Repositories:

There are various online archives and repositories that offer access to digitized Freedmen's Bureau records. These platforms may vary in terms of accessibility and subscription requirements.

Embracing the journey to unearth your African heritage is a powerful act of reclaiming a vital part of your identity. Through services like African Ancestry, you have the opportunity to trace the footsteps of your ancestors across the African continent, connecting to the roots that have shaped your family's story. Equally significant is delving into the post-emancipation era with the Freedmen's Bureau records, where stories of resilience, freedom, and aspirations await discovery. As you embark on this voyage, remember that every name you uncover and every story you reveal is a triumph over history's silences. Your quest to honor your past is a beacon for the future, inspiring generations to come. So, let the whispers of your ancestors guide you, and may your journey be filled with revelations that ignite your spirit and light your path.

Let your curiosity guide you, let your DNA illuminate your path, and answer the call of Mother Africa. Embrace the unknown with open arms, for in tracing your roots, you're breathing life into a story that has been waiting for you to tell.

Chapter Five: NARA

Discovering Your Indigenous Roots

Instructions on how to us tools for locating your Indigenous relatives starts on page 26 of Rediscovering Your Roots Companion Guide.

Dear reader, your journey to uncover your indigenous heritage is one of deep significance and connection. Embrace this adventure with open arms and a heart full of curiosity. As you turn the page, step forward with determination and a newfound understanding of the remarkable history that courses through your veins.

National Archives and Records Administration (NARA)

We're embarking on a quest to uncover your indigenous heritage – note that you are on a journey of self-discovery that bridges the past and present. Be patient and thorough in your search and be sure to approach the subject with cultural sensitivity.

Researching Indigenous genealogy can be complex and may require a combination of different records and resources with NARA being one of those sources. You'll want to explore various sections and resources that might contain relevant records. Additionally, it's recommended to verify the accuracy of records and consult with Indigenous communities when possible.

Let's dive into the fascinating world of genealogy testing, heritage recognition, and the meaningful path towards becoming a part of your tribe.

Contact Information:

Website: www.archives.gov

Telephone: 1-866-272-6272.

If you're having difficulty finding specific records, you can reach out to NARA's customer support or archives specialists for assistance.

Cost of services : <u>These services are generally free</u>, however, some services might have associated fees, such as making photocopies or scans of records.

Here are some NARA sections and resources to consider:

Research Our Records: This section of the NARA website provides access to a wide range of records, including census records, military records, and more. You can start your search by using the search bar on the homepage or by browsing through different categories.

Native American Records: NARA's "Native American Heritage" page provides information and resources related to records of Native American tribes and communities. It includes links to various collections and research guides specifically focused on Native American genealogy.

Catalog: The NARA catalog allows you to search for specific records, collections, and documents related to Indigenous people. You can use keywords related to the tribes, locations, or time periods you're interested in.

American Indian Records in the National Archives: This section provides an overview of the records related to American Indians that are held by NARA. It includes information about treaties, censuses, land records, and more.

Research Guides: NARA offers research guides that provide information on how to access specific types of records. You might find guides related to Indigenous genealogy, such as "Researching American Indian Ancestors."

Access to Archival Databases (AAD): AAD is an online resource that provides access to a selection of NARA's archival databases. It might include records related to Indigenous populations, such as censuses and rolls.

Genealogy Testing: Unveiling the Past

Imagine being able to peer into the annals of history through your own DNA. Genealogy testing is a remarkable tool that can reveal your indigenous heritage. Tests like AncestryDNA, 23andMe, and FamilyTreeDNA can analyze your DNA to identify markers associated with specific indigenous populations. They compare your results to vast databases, helping you uncover connections you might not have known existed.

<u>**For African American Readers**</u>

On January 29, 2018, in reference to the Thomasina E. Jordan Indian Tribes of Virginia Federal Recognition Act, Virginia Representative, James R. Moran said the following to the Senate Committee on Indian Affairs, "… At the time when the federal government granted Native Americans the right to vote, Virginia's elected officials adopted racially hostile laws targeted at those classes of people who did not fit into the dominant white society."

Representative Moran continued to say, "**With great hypocrisy**, Virginia's ruling elite pushed policies that culminated with the enactment of the Racial Integrity Act of 1924, an act that enforced a binary racial classification system that categorized individuals as either "White" or "Colored." The Act directed state officials, and zealots like Walter Plecker, to destroy state and local courthouse records and reclassify <u>in Orwellian fashion</u> all non-whites as "colored." It targeted Native Americans with a vengeance, denying Native Americans in Virginia their identity."

Explanation: Doing something "in Orwellian fashion" means behaving in a way that resembles the ideas and concepts found in George Orwell's book "1984." In the book, there's a society where the government watches and controls everything, distorts information, and limits people's freedoms. So, when we say something is done "in Orwellian fashion," it's like saying it's done in a way that feels like the government or authority is trying to control and manipulate what people know and think, just like in the book. It's a way of showing that something might not be honest or fair.

The Nation's First Account of Identity Theft

The adoption of the Racial Integrity Act of 1924 had a significant impact on Virginia's racial landscape, <u>leading to policies **that erased**</u> and suppressed the **<u>cultural identities</u>** of Indigenous communities.

Representative Moran stated, "… The Act did not provide separate categories for specific ethnic or cultural identities, including Native Americans. Instead, anyone who did not fit within the designated "White" category was classified as "Colored," which is what led to the erasure of diverse cultural identities and heritages. It has been called a "paper genocide."

Our ancestors were discouraged from identifying as Native Americans in Virginia because in doing so they risked a jail sentence of up to one year. However, many of our ancestors have stated through oral stories that if they were to call themselves Native American, they could have been killed.

I want to go back and speak to a statement Representative Moran made that I highlighted back on page 61. Moran stated, ".. with great hypocrisy, Virginia's ruling elite pushed policies…" The hypocrisy Moran was speaking of is the fact that Virginia's ruling elite made a claim to be blood descendants of Pocahontas, and in their view that meant that no one else in Virginia could make a claim that they were Native American and a descendant to Pocahontas' people. To do so would mean that Virginia's ruling elite were what they decreed all non-whites to be: part of "the inferior Negroid (colored) race." It's important to recognize that the Act's classification system was based on a racial hierarchy that prioritized "Whiteness" and aimed to maintain a strict separation between racial groups.

Once the elites had falsely established their "Native" heritage, they burned the city and state records so we couldn't disproved their false claims, and we wouldn't be able to rightly validate our heritage as the true descendants of Native Americans backed by census records. These supremist erased our Indigenous identity and put themselves in our place!

Dr. Walter Plecker, Virginia's Director of Vital Statistics, lead the charge in encouraging other states to follow suit. So, just like Virginia, similar laws were enacted in other states with the same results being actualized - city and state's records were destroyed due to fires and Native Americans were reclassified as "Colored."

I am giving you this brief history of reclassification because here is where your family's oral histories will be vital!

Dane Calloway: Discovering Indigenous Roots

Dane Calloway is a prominent figure known for his exploration of African American and indigenous heritage. He identifies as a "black Indian," a term used to acknowledge both his African and Native American ancestry. With a dedicated website called I'm Just Here to Make You Think ("IJHTMYT"). Dane's website, "IJHTMYT," is a hub for information and discussions surrounding the intersection of Black and indigenous heritage in America. Through videos, articles, and research, he delves into the historical complexities of these connections, shedding light on a lesser-known aspect of American history.

Many individuals, authors, and scholars are contributing to the conversation about their indigenous heritage within the Black community. Some of them include:

- Tiya Miles: An author and scholar who has written extensively about the connections between African and indigenous peoples in America.
- Kimberly TallBear: A researcher whose work explores the intersections of race, gender, and indigeneity in science and technology.
- Dr. Arica L. Coleman: A historian whose research highlights the experiences of Black and indigenous people in the United States.
- Tiffany M. Anderson: An author and advocate for Indigenous African Ancestries, exploring shared history and cultural connections.
- Ronald Smith: An activist who works to uncover the historical experiences of black Native Americans.
- Rainy Fields: A writer and activist discussing the Afro-Indigenous experience in America.

These voices, along with Dane Calloway's efforts, contribute to a growing awareness of the Black community connecting to their indigenous cultures and reclaiming lost narratives.

Below is a strategic plan that can aid you when you begin searching for your family's Indigenous files.

1. **Research Plan:** Define your research goals and create a plan. Determine what information you already have and what you're hoping to discover about your indigenous background.

2. **Visit the National Archives:** Identify which branch of the National Archives you should visit. The National Archives and Records Administration (NARA) has locations throughout the United States. Check their website for the nearest location to you.

3. **Online Resources:** Explore the National Archives website for online databases, resources, and research guides related to indigenous records. They provide access to records related to Native American tribes, treaties, land records, and more.

4. **Census Records:** Census records can be particularly useful. The U.S. Federal Census included information about individuals' ethnicity, including indigenous identities. Look for census records that correspond to the time periods your ancestors lived.

5. **Treaty Records:** The National Archives holds treaties between the U.S. government and indigenous tribes. These documents can offer insights into tribal affiliations and historical interactions.

6. **Dawes Rolls and Enrollment Records:** If your family has connections to Native American tribes that were subject to enrollment, the Dawes Rolls and similar records can provide information about tribal membership.

7. **Land Records:** Land records might contain details about land allotments or ownership related to indigenous heritage.

8. **Correspondence and Documents:** Explore correspondence, letters, and other documents that might mention indigenous ancestry. Government

documents, personal letters, and military records can sometimes hold clues.

9. **Request Assistance:** If you're unable to visit a National Archives location in person, you can request assistance from archivists or researchers. They can help you identify relevant records and guide your research remotely.

10. **Respect Cultural Sensitivity:** Remember that researching indigenous heritage requires cultural sensitivity. Approach the research with respect for the communities and their histories.

11. **Consult with Experts:** If you encounter challenges or want more guidance, consider consulting with genealogists or researchers who specialize in indigenous genealogy.

12. **Visit Tribal Resources:** Indigenous tribes often have their own archives, museums, and resources. Check if the tribe you're researching has its own historical documentation available to the public.

Remember that finding indigenous heritage can be complex, and records might not always be comprehensive or easily accessible. It's important to approach research with patience and an open mind.

MY INSPIRATIONAL STORY

Cherry's Legacy: Unearthing Our Roots

In the heart of our family's history lies a story that weaves together the threads of generations, connecting us to a remarkable past. This is a tale of validation, of tracing back our ancestry through time to an Indigenous woman named Cherry, who whispered the secrets of her heritage into the winds of history.

Mary's Legacy: The Spark that Ignited Me

My great grandmother, Mary, was a storyteller who breathed life into our family's history. She spoke of Cherry, her grandmother, with a sense of pride that echoed through the years. Cherry, she whispered, was Native American.

In the heart of our family's history lies a tale of whispered stories, unspoken truths, and a journey that led us to uncover Cherry, an ancestor whose heritage we yearned to confirm.

Oral Histories: Glimpses of Cherry's Journey

From the stories passed down through hushed conversations, we heard the faint echoes of our ancestors. Mary, my great grandmother, spoke of Cherry, her grandmother, who was said to have come from the Dakotas during the harrowing days of slavery. These tales were threads of connection, sewing together the stories of a past that had been shrouded in the mists of time. Mary's words held a magic that tugged at my curiosity, urging me to uncover the truth.

Yet, as I delved deeper, I found the tapestry of our history woven with gaps. Mary's stories were our guideposts, but they led us to an uncertain crossroads. While her whispers spoke of the Dakotas. We heard rumors of our family's ties to the Black Hills, a sacred land that seemed to hold our secrets close. But the exact tribe remained elusive.

A Census Declaration: Cherry's Bold Truth

Amidst the fog of uncertainty, a glimmer of truth emerged from a page of history. The year was 1900, and there, etched in ink, was Cherry's name on a census form. Next to the question of her race, she had declared herself as "Cha

Nook." There on this fragile piece of paper, in handwriting, was Cherry's name, and beside it, her declaration. It was a whispered truth, preserved in ink on that fragile sheet, waiting for someone to pick up the threads and follow them.

Despite the threat of jail time or death, Cherry made a stand. What was even more surprising is that the census enumerator and city officials allowed her declaration to be recorded.

With Cherry's declaration as my guide, I turned my gaze towards the Chinook Native Americans. As I waded through historical records and woven narratives, I unearthed the Chinook people, who were known for their tenacious spirit and business acumen.

Echoes of Lewis and Clark

As I delved into the history of the Chinook people, I found myself standing on the shores of discovery. Lewis and Clark had written about them in their journals. They marveled at their resourcefulness, their culture, and their way of life. They wrote of the Chinook people's warring spirit and their intricate dealings with the newcomers. The pages of history darkened as I read about the Chinookans

71

trade practices and commerce, which was marred by the shadows of slavery, as the Chinook sold war captives into servitude—a chilling reminder of the complexity of history.

Note: As a tactic, many European trade negotiators whispered in the ears of tribal elders and warned them that their captives would one day rise up against them. They persuaded them to trade their war captives in exchange for guns. That pitched this as a win-win scenario. The tribes would have gunpower to fight of the warring tribes, and the colonizers would have the bodies they needed for slavery.

As I embarked on my journey to unearth my indigenous heritage, I realized that within every whispered story, there's a world waiting to be uncovered. Each thread of history weaved into the tapestry of our lives holds the power to connect us to a past rich with stories, struggles, and triumphs. Your own heritage, much like mine, might be a puzzle with missing pieces, waiting for you to seek out and assemble. Embrace the magic of discovery, and with curiosity as your guide, venture forth into the unknown. Your ancestors' whispers, just like mine, have stories to share, and it's within your grasp to unveil them. So, take that step, and embark on a journey that promises to illuminate the path that leads you back to your roots.

I authored a novel drawing upon the knowledge I gained about my ancestors. To get a copy of my book scan the QR code or follow the link below. Once there, like, share & comment. Don't forget to turn on your notifications to get notified about current posts and tutorials.

www.facebook.com/TheCedarChest23

If you're excited to explore your indigenous heritage, reach out to recognized tribes directly. They can guide you through the process of tracing your ancestry, confirming your heritage, and possibly becoming a member. You can find contact information on official tribe websites or through organizations dedicated to indigenous affairs, such as the National Congress of American Indians.

Website: https://www.ncai.org.

Phone number: 202-466-7767.

Costs: NCAI offers memberships to tribes, tribal organizations, and individual members. Membership fees may apply, and the cost can vary depending on the type of membership and the size of the entity joining.

The Native Land Wand Maps Website

The Native Land website is an interactive online platform that provides maps illustrating the traditional territories and ancestral lands of Indigenous peoples around the world. The website allows users to explore and learn about the historical and contemporary presence of Indigenous tribes and nations on a global scale.

The Native Land website: http://native-land.ca

The maps on the Native Land website use color-coded overlays to depict different Indigenous territories, languages, and cultural groups. Users can input specific addresses or geographical locations to see which Indigenous groups historically inhabited or currently inhabit those areas.

Native Land Digital, the organization behind the Native Land Maps website (native-land.ca), does not typically provide direct contact information on their website. However, they do have a presence on social media platforms like Twitter, Instagram, and Facebook, where you might be able to reach out or find updates about their work.

For the most current contact information or any inquiries you may have, you can visit the Native Land Maps website and look for any contact details they may have provided or explore their social media presence for updates.

This resource is often used by individuals seeking to learn more about the Indigenous history and connections to specific regions. It's a tool for increasing awareness about Indigenous presence and for acknowledging the complex histories of the land we live on.

Keep in mind that while the Native Land website is a valuable educational resource, it might not replace in-depth genealogical research if you're seeking specific ancestral information. It's important to use the website alongside other reputable sources and engage with Indigenous communities with respect and cultural sensitivity.

In conclusion, if you're yearning to learn more about your indigenous heritage, Library of Congress (LOC) and the National Archives are invaluable resources. Websites like Native Land and Tribal Nations Maps provide interactive maps that outline indigenous territories. Recognized tribes, like the Cherokee, Navajo, and Sioux, for example, have their own websites that offer historical information and resources.

Benefits of Heritage Confirmation

Discovering and confirming your indigenous heritage isn't just about the past – it's about embracing your identity and connecting with a community that shares your history. Becoming a member of a recognized tribe can bring a sense of belonging and unity. It opens the door to cultural traditions, ceremonies, and a supportive network that celebrates your journey.

Reparations and Seeking Justice

Reparations vary from tribe to tribe and often include benefits like access to educational scholarships, healthcare services, and cultural preservation programs. The possibility of reparations for historical injustices is a complex matter that depends on individual tribe policies, government recognition, and ongoing efforts for justice.

Dear reader, as we traverse this journey of validation and discovery, let us walk hand in hand with our ancestors. Each step we take, each <u>word</u> we uncover, becomes a bridge between our past and our present.

Chapter Six: Oral Histories

Weaving in Stories

Suggestions on how to collect stories starts on page 34 of Rediscovering Your Roots Companion Guide.

Oh, the joy of sitting down with Aunt Bernice or Uncle James to listen to their tales! Oral histories are like family secrets wrapped in warmth and humor. They hold gems that no document or record can capture. Grab your notepad, your recording device, or just a cup of tea and start chatting. Record their memories, the triumphs, the trials, and the sweet moments that make your family's story unique. Cherish these conversations like the treasures they are.

Collecting Oral Stories

Gather 'round, fellow storytellers, for in the corners of our family elders' homes lie the treasures of our heritage, tucked away in shoeboxes, family Bibles, and cedar chests. These humble repositories hold stories of our ancestors, waiting to be discovered, cherished, and woven into the tapestry of our family's history.

Visiting Elders: Guardians of Treasured Documents

Picture yourself sitting with your elder relatives, their eyes twinkling with the wisdom of years gone by. As you listen to their stories, you might find that they possess more than just memories. Delve a little deeper, and you might unearth shoeboxes brimming with photographs, letters, and forgotten documents.

These shoeboxes are like time capsules, carrying the essence of our ancestors' lives. Each photograph captures a moment in their journey, every letter a window into their thoughts and emotions. These relics were carefully preserved by our elders, entrusted to them as guardians of our family's legacy.

Family Bibles: Portals of Connection

Ah, the family Bible – more than just a book, it's a binding force that transcends generations. Within its pages, births, marriages, and deaths are recorded, forming a thread that weaves through time. This treasured tome is more than ink on paper; it's a portal that connects us to our ancestors, allowing us to touch the same pages they touched, to read the same words they read.

Imagine the significance of discovering your great-grandmother's handwriting, marking the day your grandparent was born. The family Bible is a testament to the importance of continuity, a place where the past and present converge in an unbroken chain.

Cedar Chests: Guardians of History

Cedar chests, like sentinels of our past, stand as guardians of history. Within their aromatic embrace lie the secrets of generations – letters, diaries, legal documents, and heirlooms that have been passed down through time. These chests were more than storage; they were vessels of love and protection, shielding our ancestors' stories from the ravages of time.

Opening a cedar chest is like stepping into a time capsule. You might find love letters exchanged decades ago, or a certificate that tells the story of your ancestor's achievements. With each touch of these delicate papers, you bridge the gap between past and present, becoming a conduit for the legacy they carried.

As we explore these repositories of memory, we honor the dedication of our elders and the foresight of our ancestors. Every photograph, every document, every faded page is a link that binds us to our family's narrative. So, whether you're sifting through a shoebox, flipping through a family Bible, or unlocking the secrets of a cedar chest, know that you're preserving more than just paper and ink – you're safeguarding the essence of who you are, and the stories that make your family's journey uniquely yours.

Unveiling Hidden Treasures: Capturing Oral Histories

Hey, storyteller extraordinaire! Ready to step into the world of oral history and preserve the magical tales of your family? We're about to dive into a journey where words become bridges to the past, connecting you with the ancestors who shaped your world. So, let's roll up our sleeves and get started!

Slave Narratives

The Works Progress Administration (WPA) Slave Narratives are an invaluable collection of oral histories that provide a unique and unparalleled insight into the lives, experiences, and perspectives of African American enslaved individuals. These narratives stand as a testament to the resilience, strength, and humanity of those who endured one of the darkest periods in American history.

The WPA Slave Narratives were part of the Federal Writers' Project during the Great Depression, aimed at providing employment for writers while capturing the stories of those who had lived through slavery. The narratives were collected from the 1930s to the early 1940s and cover a wide range of topics, including daily life, family, work, religious practices, and memories of emancipation.

What makes these narratives so significant is that they preserve the voices of those who had lived through slavery, offering a direct link to a past that might otherwise have been lost. These firsthand accounts dispel myths, challenge stereotypes, and provide a counter-narrative to the distorted and dehumanizing portrayals of African Americans during slavery.

For African American genealogists and historians, the WPA Slave Narratives are a treasure trove of information. They often include names of ancestors, details about family relationships, locations, and personal anecdotes that shed light on the conditions and challenges faced by enslaved people. This information can be invaluable for tracing family histories and building a more complete picture of one's heritage.

The WPA Slave Narratives not only enrich our understanding of history but also serve as a powerful reminder of the strength of the human spirit in the face of adversity. They give a voice to those who were silenced and overlooked for far too long. As a genealogist, researcher, or anyone interested in African American history, exploring these narratives can be a profound and moving experience, connecting you with the stories of those who came before and allowing their voices to resonate across time.

Your storytelling journey is taking you to incredible heights, where documents and tales converge to create a more complete picture of your family's history. You're a historian, a listener, and a curator of memories all rolled into one. Keep celebrating the magic of oral history, and let your discoveries shine like stars in the night sky!

Chapter Seven: Navigating Challenges

There's Light Throughout the Tunnel

Tips on how to destress starts on page 40 in the Rediscovering Your Roots Companion Guide.

Let's keep it real - genealogy isn't always smooth sailing. Sometimes, you hit brick walls and roadblocks. But fear not, dear adventurer! Every frustration you encounter is a testament to your determination. Take a deep breath, step away for a moment, and then come back with fresh eyes. Seek help from genealogy communities, share your roadblocks, and watch as fellow adventurers rally to your aid.

Breaking Through Brick Walls: Seeking Expert Help

As you delve into the depths of genealogy, it's normal to encounter roadblocks and unexpected twists. Don't worry – you've got this! When frustrations knock on your door, let them in and tackle them head-on while keeping your spirits high.

When the genealogy maze gets tricky, it's time to call in the experts. Reach out to genealogy companies that offer research assistance, such as Ancestry ProGenealogists, or Legacy Tree Genealogists. These pros are like the Gandalfs of the genealogy world, guiding you through challenges.

Contact Information for Ancestry ProGenealogist:

Website: www.progenealogists.com

Phone: 1-800-596-3230

Costs: They will develop a research plan and work directly with your designated Client Relationship Manager. Prices start at $3,500 for 20 hours of research.

Contact information for Legacy Tree Genealogist

Website: legacytree.com

Phone: 1-800-818-1476

Costs: They offer full-service research packages <u>starting at</u> <u>$2,950 on to $5,600 on to $10,800</u>. The packages are priced according to researching 1, 2, and 4 research goals, respectively. They complete most projects in 4-6 months without sacrificing our commitment to exceptional research.

Genealogy services often come with costs but think of it as investing in your family's legacy. Prices can vary, so it's a good idea to research beforehand. Genealogy services may charge by the hour or offer package deals. Remember, each investment brings you closer to your ancestors' stories.

Breaking Through Brick Walls: Doing It Yourself

Harness the Power of Local Libraries

Local libraries are like hidden gems of genealogy. Their genealogy departments are treasure troves of local records, newspapers, and resources. Plus, they often offer workshops and assistance. Drop by your library's genealogy department or check out their online resources – you might find a missing puzzle piece!

Connecting with the Library of Congress Staff

Contacting Library of Congress staff can be like reaching out to history guides. They're knowledgeable and friendly, eager to assist your journey. Visit their Contact Us page to get in touch and inquire about specific records or resources that can deepen your exploration.

African American Readers

Acknowledging America's Dark Past

As an African American, your genealogy journey may lead to stories of slavery. This chapter of history is painful, but it's crucial to remember that it doesn't define you. Your ancestors' resilience and strength shine brighter than any darkness. Facing this history allows you to honor their stories while creating a better future.

The Art of Journaling

Imagine journaling as a time capsule for your emotions. When you hit a roadblock or uncover disheartening facts, jot down your thoughts. It's like venting to a trusted friend who listens without judgment. Journaling can help you process your feelings and celebrate your progress.

Walking Away and Taking Breaks

Genealogy is a marathon, not a sprint. When frustration knocks, it's okay to step back and take a breather. Go for a walk, indulge in a hobby, or simply enjoy a good book.

Stepping away refreshes your mind, so when you return, you'll be ready to conquer those challenges.

Banishing Shame and Dealing with Anger

Unearthing family stories might bring up emotions you didn't expect. Shame or anger might knock on your door, but remember, these emotions are like passing clouds. Seek support from friends, family, or even professional counselors. You're not alone on this journey.

Embrace Every Step

Remember, genealogy is about uncovering the multifaceted tapestry of your family's history. Every discovery is a victory and challenge – adds depth to that tapestry. Be kind to yourself, embrace the journey, and hold your ancestors' stories close to your heart.

My Story Time: The Quest for the Newspaper Founder

I once heard whispers of a relative who had started a Black newspaper, but the story seemed elusive, like a ghost from the past. No one knew the name of the newspaper, nor could anyone validate his ownership. It was important to me to find out all the details because it was rumored that this elder was also murdered for printing articles that was relevant to the Black community, especially pertaining to Jim Crow laws.

I was very frustrated about the cold trail until I met Ms. Rhonda, a remarkable librarian at my local library's genealogy department.

Ms. Rhonda dove into the archives for me. She was like a history detective, combing through digital archives or stacks of old newspapers and faded documents. After some searching, she uncovered the truth: my relative had indeed founded a groundbreaking newspaper that championed the African American community.

Ms. Rhonda's dedication and expertise transformed a family rumor into a concrete piece of history. Her assistance showed me the magic that happens when passion meets knowledge, turning forgotten stories into tangible realities.

You're crafting a legacy, piecing together stories that span generations. As you face frustrations and find solutions, know that your journey is a testament to your dedication and love for your family's history. The past is rooting for you, and you're creating a bridge between it and the future. Keep shining!

Chapter Eight: Guided by Ancestral Whispers

◆

You Were Always There

A list of typical signs starts on page 44 in the
Rediscovering Your Roots Companion Guide.

Your journey is like a symphony, orchestrated by your ancestors and guided by synchronicities. The threads of the past and present intertwine, revealing stories that were meant to be uncovered. So, keep following those whispers, those tugs at your heart, and remember that your ancestors are by your side, every step of the way.

A Journey of Synchronicities and Reconnections

As you've delved deeper into your genealogy journey, have you ever felt like your ancestors were leading you, guiding your steps through time? Well, get ready for some heartwarming tales of synchronicity and connection that will leave you awe-struck.

Ancestral Whispers and Synchronicities

Ever had that feeling that your ancestors are whispering in your ear, urging you forward? It's like they're guiding your steps through history, revealing hidden treasures along the way. Embrace those goosebumps – your ancestors are your compass, leading you to your roots.

My Story: The Facebook Genealogy Miracle

I once joined a Facebook genealogy group called "I've Traced My Enslaved Ancestors and Their Owners." It was like stepping into a community of fellow explorers.

I had been a member for only a few days when I decided to post a question. I had a labor contract, and I could not decipher the name of the plantation owner. Within minutes I had over 40 responses. It was crystal clear was they called out the name, so much so, that I can't explain why I couldn't read it on my own.

Minutes after posting my request for assistance, these genealogy wizards began posting more in our chat. I'll be honest with you, it was distracting. I was trying to continue my writing and I kept hearing chiming bells every time someone posted. So, I decided to take a look. I thought it would be about someone else's question. Boy, was I need for a treat. The group had continued to discuss my question. It was as if the virtual universe conspired to help me uncover my family's history.

Here's what happened, a member of the group posted a report in our chat. The report provided insight on my enslaver's town. Then another member posted a historical report about prominent people in the town which include my ancestor's enslaver. Out of respect for their research, I read the section in report that the member directed me to.

Let me share a little background, months before asking the Facebook group for help, I had reconnected with a cousin, whom I hadn't spoken to in over 30 years. She and I laughed and reconnected like time had stood still. Our bonds had maintained their strength. We shared our life journeys with each other and vowed to stay in touch.

Now here is where the story gets even more incredible. A few weeks after the Facebook group had found my ancestor's enslaver and the town he resided in; my teen daughter was offered a director position for a dance camp after the standing director resigned. I volunteered to drive her because it was a long distance. On our departure day, I called my long-lost cousin again. To my surprise she was headed to a city that was only 82 miles from where we were. My cousin invited us to stay the weekend with them at their Airbnb, so our children could get to meet and bond.

We met in Texas, and here's the mind-blowing part come in; it was half a mile from where my ancestor was enslaved. It was like my ancestors had orchestrated the meeting, weaving a tapestry of reconnection, and belonging.

What made it so incredible was that had our rendezvous point been just a quarter of a mile sooner in distance, I would have never seen the name of a former slave which bared the name of my ancestor's enslaver. It was only when I saw the name of the cemetery that I realized I was in the town that I had written on the historical report.

Remember, interpreting signs is highly personal and can vary from person to person. What matters most is the meaning and comfort these signs bring to your journey. Whether you see them as messages from ancestors, the universe, or a higher power, these signs can provide guidance, solace, and a sense of connection to those who came before us.

Chapter Nine:
Collecting Artifacts

Requesting Files from Family Historians

Guidance on storing files starts on page 48 in the
Rediscovering Your Roots Companion Guide.

Preserving historical files is not just an act of safeguarding the past; it's a profound commitment to honoring the stories that have shaped us. Each document, photograph, and artifact carries a piece of our shared history, a link to our roots, and a testament to the lives that have come before us.

Requesting Files

In the grand tapestry of your family's history, each member holds a unique piece of the puzzle. But danger lurks when these pieces remain scattered, hidden in forgotten albums or carried only by individual memories. Like a mosaic missing crucial tiles, our shared heritage can become fragmented, leaving gaps in our understanding. Even among siblings, treasured photographs and untold stories disperse, creating a fractured narrative. Extended families, too, often carry only the echoes of their own branches, missing out on the grand symphony of our collective journey.

Yet, in this digital age, we have the power to weave our history back together. The importance of capturing our entire story cannot be overstated. Our shared roots deserve a united tapestry, a tale that resonates through every branch and leaf of our family tree. Imagine a central depository, a digital haven where every contribution finds a home. No longer will there be a whisper of history denied to one branch while another flourishes with knowledge. Instead, we create a legacy of inclusivity, where every member has access to the stories, images, and memories that define us.

Let this be our mission: to honor the fragments that each family member holds and assemble them into a masterpiece that spans generations. In this endeavor, we pledge to safeguard our heritage, not just for ourselves, but for every cousin, aunt, and nephew. Together, we will bridge the gaps, erase the voids, and breathe life into the forgotten whispers of the past. For in unity, our family's story gains strength, becoming an enduring legacy that all can proudly claim as their own.

Approach Your Elders With Reverence!

In the delicate tapestry of shared history, your role as the historian and keeper of treasures is profoundly respected and will be honored. As you embark on a journey to weave your family's stories together, approach your relatives with a humble request. Let them know that you understand that the photographs, letters, and documents they hold are not just mere artifacts, but they are precious threads that connect to their and your roots.

Express to them that with utmost respect and care, you are asking for their permission to scan or copy their invaluable pieces of the family's heritage.

Provide assurance to your elders and keepers of family history that you recognize that these artifacts have been lovingly preserved by their hands, passed down through generations, and you recognize that it holds a piece of their heart. Assure them that your intention is to honor and safeguard these treasures, to preserve them for future generations to come.

I recommend giving your elders some assurance, here's an example text – " ... *I will treat your documents with the reverence they deserve, that they will be returned to you unharmed and unaltered. Your stories, your memories, and your love for our family are the threads that have woven us into who we are today. We want to ensure that your legacy lives on, shared with the respect and admiration it deserves. My mission is not only to compile these pieces into a grand narrative but to also ensure that your role as a steward of our history is celebrated and appreciated. We understand the weight of this request and extend our gratitude for entrusting us with these invaluable heirlooms. Your wisdom, your memories, and your guidance are a guiding light on this journey, and we are immensely grateful for your presence in our lives.*

By valuing and protecting family treasures you are bridging a gap between generations, ensuring that the narratives of your ancestors continue to inspire, educate, and guide the family. As guardians of our heritage, let us stand united in the effort to keep the echoes of history alive, so that the wisdom of the past may light the way for the future.

Chapter Ten: Sharing Your Story

—◆—

Telling the World

Post-research Instructions starts on page 56 in the Rediscovering Your Roots Companion Guide.

Congratulations, dear explorer, you've embarked on a journey that has unveiled the rich tapestry of your family's history. As you stand on the threshold of becoming your family's next storyteller, know that you hold the key to a legacy that spans generations. But remember, your newfound treasures shouldn't be hidden away in a shoebox; they deserve to shine as the centerpiece of a masterpiece — your very own family history book or nonfiction novel.

Commercializing the Fruits of your Labor

Congratulations, fearless genealogist! You've journeyed through the digital alleys of ancestry.com, time-traveled with the Library of Congress, identified any African and/or Indigenous roots you may have, and gathered the cherished stories of your kin. Your family's history is now more vivid and alive than ever before. As you continue to uncover more stories, remember that the past is a puzzle with infinite pieces. Embrace the thrilling moments and the challenging ones. Your ancestors are cheering you on from the shadows, grateful that you're preserving their legacy.

You've gathered treasures from the past, but why stop there? Let your creativity flow and consider writing a book about your family's history. Blend your findings with your own voice to create a tapestry of stories. It's like becoming a storyteller for your ancestors, sharing their triumphs, heartaches, and adventures.

Writing a book about your family's history is a wonderful endeavor that can leave a lasting legacy for generations to come. Here are some encouraging words to inspire you on this rewarding journey:

Remember, you're not just writing a book; you're capturing the heartbeats of your ancestors, sharing their triumphs and struggles with the world. Your journey has been a testament to perseverance and discovery. As you step into the role of your family's storyteller, let your voice resound through time, illuminating the stories that deserve to be heard. Here's to your future as a published author, a legacy builder, and a beacon of inspiration for generations to come!

Writing a book about your family's history is a gift to yourself and to those who will follow. Your dedication to preserving these stories is a testament to the love and respect you have for your ancestors. Embrace this journey with joy, curiosity, and the knowledge that your efforts will make a lasting impact on your family's legacy.

———◆———

To check out my family history book, go to:

https://instagram.com/themilelegroup?igshid =NjIwNzIyMDk2Mg==

I will periodically host how-to tutorials on writing family history books using facts found during genealogical searches. I will offer valuable advice, inspiration, and practical tools to help you navigate the process of writing and completing your book, so follow me on my social media and turn your notifications on.

Below is a list of books that offer guidance on writing a book, covering various aspects of the writing process, from getting started to polishing your manuscript:

- "The Elements of Story: Field Notes on Nonfiction Writing" by Francis Flaherty.
  It is a comprehensive guide to crafting engaging and impactful nonfiction stories, with insights on structure, character, and narrative.
- "The Anatomy of Story: 22 Steps to Becoming a Master Storyteller" by John Truby.
  A comprehensive guide to story structure, character development, and creating compelling narratives.
- "The Writing Life" by Annie Dillard.
  A reflection on the challenges and joys of a writer's journey, offering insights into the creative process and the dedication required.
- "You Are a Writer (So Start Acting Like One)" by Jeff Goins.
  A motivational book that encourages aspiring writers to embrace their identity as writers and take actionable steps toward their goals.

Different books may resonate with different writers, so consider a few that align with your writing style and goals.

Representation for Your book: Getting A Literary Agent

Literary agents will represent you as an author and shop around to get your book published. They work off commission. The standard commission rate is around **15%** of the author's advance and royalties.

Here's how it works:

<u>Advance</u>: When a publisher offers you a publishing contract, they often provide an advance payment against future royalties. This advance is typically paid in installments: upon signing the contract, upon acceptance of the manuscript, and upon publication.

<u>Royalties</u>: After your book is published and starts generating sales, you'll earn royalties based on a percentage of each sale. Royalty rates can vary depending on the format (hardcover, paperback, eBook) and sales channel.

The agent's commission is usually calculated as a percentage of both the advance and the ongoing royalties. Here's a breakdown:

<u>Advance Commission</u>: Let's say your advance is $10,000, and your agent's commission rate is 15%. Your agent would receive 15% of the $10,000 advance, which is $1,500.

Royalty Commission: As your book sells and generates royalties, your agent continues to receive a 15% commission on the royalties you earn from book sales.

Note that while agents typically receive a percentage of your earnings, they play a significant role in negotiating favorable contracts, providing guidance throughout the publishing process, and advocating for your interests.

Before signing with an agent, it's essential to discuss and clarify the terms of the agency agreement, including the commission rate and any other fees. Literary agent practices and commission rates can vary, so be sure to have a transparent conversation to ensure you're both on the same page.

Self-Publishing:

It's an empowering avenue that gives you full control. Platforms like Amazon Kindle Direct Publishing and IngramSpark offer step-by-step guides to help you transform your manuscript into a published work of art.

Please note that contact information and procedures might change over time. To get the most accurate and up-to-date information, I recommend visiting each print providers websites.

Choose a Publishing Platform: Research and select a self-publishing platform such as Amazon Kindle Direct Publishing (KDP), IngramSpark, 48HourBooks, or others.

Amazon Kindle Direct Publishing (KDP)

Amazon KDP is a platform for self-publishing eBooks and print books:

Website: https://kdp.amazon.com/

Customer Support:

For customer support inquiries, log in to your KDP account and click on the "Help" link in the upper-right corner. You'll find options to contact their support team via email or chat.

Amazon KDP does not typically provide a direct phone number for customer support. Most inquiries are handled through their online support system.

You can use the "Contact Us" form within your KDP account to send an email inquiry.

IngramSpark

IngramSpark is a platform that provides print-on-demand and eBook distribution services for self-published authors:

Website: https://www.ingramspark.com/

For customer support inquiries, you can visit their support page: https://www.ingramspark.com/how-it-works/support

They provide a contact form for inquiries and support requests.

Phone: 1-855-99SPARK (1-855-997-7275) (United States)

International: +44 1235 465500 (United Kingdom)

You can find email contact options on their support page based on your location and the type of inquiry.

48 Hour Books

48 Hour Books is a company that provides printing services for books:

Website: https://www.48hrbooks.com/

For customer support inquiries, you can visit their customer service page:

https://www.48hrbooks.com/contact-us

They have a print calculator which allows you to see costs associated with the book you want.

Customer Service: 1-800-231-0521 (United States)

International: +1-330-677-4025

Email: General Inquiries: info@48hrbooks.com

Email: Order Inquiries: orders@48hrbooks.com

Traditional Publishing vs. Self-Publishing

Choosing between traditional publishing and self-publishing is a crossroads moment. Traditional publishing offers wider distribution and marketing support, but it can be competitive. Self-publishing empowers you to control your book's journey, but it requires more hands-on work for marketing.

Publishing Platforms and Distribution

Your book deserves a wide reach, and platforms like Amazon, Barnes & Noble, and IngramSpark can help you achieve that. Distribute your book both digitally and in print formats to make it accessible to readers worldwide.

Your First Book Signing Event

Imagine your name adorning your very first book cover. A book signing event can be a celebration of your journey. Plan your event by finding a suitable venue, inviting friends and family, and preparing readings or presentations that resonate with your book's themes.

Making Money via Streaming

When your screenplay is adapted and produced into a television show or movie that is streamed on platforms like Netflix, Hulu, or other streaming services, you can potentially earn money through various avenues. Here's how you can make money from your screenplay's adaptation:

Option Fee:

When a production company or studio decides to adapt your screenplay, they usually pay an option fee. This fee grants them the exclusive right to develop and produce the adaptation for a specific period of time.

Purchase Price:

If the adaptation moves forward and gets the green light for production, you'll receive a purchase price. This is a larger sum that reflects the full acquisition of the rights to your screenplay.

Screenwriter's Fee:

If you're hired to work on the adaptation as a screenwriter, you'll receive a fee for your writing services. This may include revisions, rewrites, and any additional work on the script.

Royalties or Backend Compensation:

Depending on the terms of your contract, you may be entitled to royalties or backend compensation. This involves a percentage of the profits generated by the show or movie, which could come from subscription fees, advertising revenue, international sales, and more.

Producer Credit and Fees:

If you're involved in the production process as an executive producer, you may receive additional compensation and credits.

Residuals:

Residuals are ongoing payments made to writers and other key creative contributors when the adaptation is rerun on the platform or released on other media formats, such as DVDs or international broadcasts.

Bonuses and Incentives:

Some contracts include bonuses based on factors like ratings, critical acclaim, or awards received by the adaptation.

Syndication and International Sales:

If the adaptation is sold to other networks or platforms domestically or internationally, you may receive additional income from these sales.

Merchandising and Ancillary Rights:

If your adaptation leads to merchandise, video games, spin-offs, or other related projects, you could earn money from these ancillary rights.

It's important to note that the specifics of your compensation will depend on the terms negotiated in your contract with the production company, studio, or streaming platform. Entertainment contracts can be complex, so it's advisable to have an entertainment attorney review and negotiate your contract to ensure you're being fairly compensated for your work.

While the potential for financial gain exists, not all adaptations guarantee substantial income, and the success of the project can influence your earnings. Regardless, having your screenplay adapted and seen on popular streaming platforms can provide exposure, career opportunities, and the satisfaction of seeing your story come to life.

Contacting Netflix

Contacting Netflix as an individual screenwriter or content creator can be challenging, as they primarily work with established production companies, agents, and industry professionals. However, you can still explore certain avenues to potentially pitch your ideas or get noticed:

Work with an Agent:

Literary agents with connections in the entertainment industry can help pitch your screenplay to production companies and studios, including those that work with Netflix.

Pitch Festivals and Contests:

Participate in pitch festivals or screenwriting contests that offer opportunities to showcase your work to industry professionals. Winning or placing in these events might attract attention.

Online Platforms:

Some platforms, like the Black List, offer services to help writers share their scripts with industry professionals, including those from Netflix.

Networking:

Attend film festivals, industry events, and workshops to network with professionals in the entertainment industry who might have connections to Netflix.

Online Platforms and Forums:

Engage in online forums, social media groups, and websites where industry professionals discuss various aspects of the entertainment business. You might make valuable connections.

Submit to Production Companies:

Research production companies that have a history of working with streaming platforms like Netflix. Submit your screenplay to these companies directly.

Remember that Netflix primarily works with experienced professionals and established production companies. While it might be challenging to contact them directly as an individual, pursuing the options above can increase your chances of getting noticed by industry professionals who have connections to Netflix or other streaming platforms. Always ensure that you're submitting your work in a professional and polished manner.

The Silver Screen

Navigating Hollywood's labyrinth might seem daunting, but it's a step-by-step process. Pitch your screenplay to producers, attend industry events, and network with fellow creatives. The path to landing a movie deal on streaming services like Netflix or Hulu is paved with persistence and passion.

As you stand on the precipice of your ancestral journey, armed with the wisdom of the past and the tools of the present, remember that the quest to rediscover your roots is a testament to your unwavering curiosity and resilience.

By immersing yourself into trusted resources, you've embarked on a path that leads not only to names and dates, but to the beating heart of your family's history.

The steps you take, the stories you uncover, and the connections you forge will paint a vivid portrait of the tapestry that is your lineage.

If you need step-by-step instruction, tips, and/or guidance to aid you in this historical journey, consider acquiring the companion guide to this book and the workbook.

Rediscovering Your Roots: Companion Guide: Step-by-Step Instructions to Finding Your Ancestors, is a compass to navigate the intricate terrain of genealogical exploration; and

Rediscovering Your Roots Workbook, is a workbook which list questions you should ask when interviewing elders/relatives.

As you embark on this quest armed with knowledge and fueled by determination, remember that every piece of your heritage you unearth is a tribute to your ancestors and an indelible mark upon your own story.

With your heart as your guide and history as your muse, embrace the joy of discovery, for each step forward is a step toward rediscovering not only your roots, but also the essence of who you are. Happy hunting, and may your journey be as illuminating as it is fulfilling.

A round of applause, please!

It's time to revel in your achievements. Whether you've traced your lineage back five generations or simply connected with a long-lost cousin, every step is a triumph. Frame that photograph you found or proudly display your family tree. Remember, genealogy is about embracing your history and honoring the journey.

Words from the Author

Embrace the journey of rediscovery with unwavering determination. As you venture into the depths of history, remember that every step you take brings you closer to your roots, your identity, and a profound connection to the past. Doubt may try to cloud your path, disturbing facts may challenge your resolve, and naysayers may question your pursuit, but within you lies a fire that cannot be extinguished. Your efforts today are the foundation for the legacies of tomorrow. Let the stories of your ancestors be your guide, for they whisper in the wind, urging you onward. With courage in your heart and curiosity as your compass, take this journey, for in embracing your past, you shape a brighter future for all who follow in your footsteps.

If you want to learn more about me and my works you can follow me on my social media. Once there, don't forget to like, share, and comment.

https://instagram.com/themilelegroup?igshid=NjIwNzIyMDk2Mg==

www.facebook.com/TheCedarChest23

About the Author

Subrena C. Bowers is an author whose life's chapters are as diverse as her passions. As a devoted mother of three girls, her nurturing spirit extends to both her family and her craft. With over 35 years as a technical grant writer, Subrena's  eloquence has bridged countless ideas and initiatives, a testament to her talent for articulating complexity with clarity. Alongside her professional journey, she is an avid amateur genealogist, crafting narratives that resurrect the stories of ancestors in her acclaimed history trilogy "We Are Milele" volumes I, II, and III. Committed to truth and exploration, she penned the nonfiction gem "The Cedar Chest," drawing readers into a world meticulously built upon research. Beyond words, Subrena finds solace in the harmony of jazz, the canvas of art, and the boundless realm of writing.

In Subrena Bowers' tapestry of identity, the threads of motherhood, wordsmithing, and a love for heritage weave together, painting a portrait of a woman who cherishes every nuance of life's melody.

9 798218 537326